The Wor ver

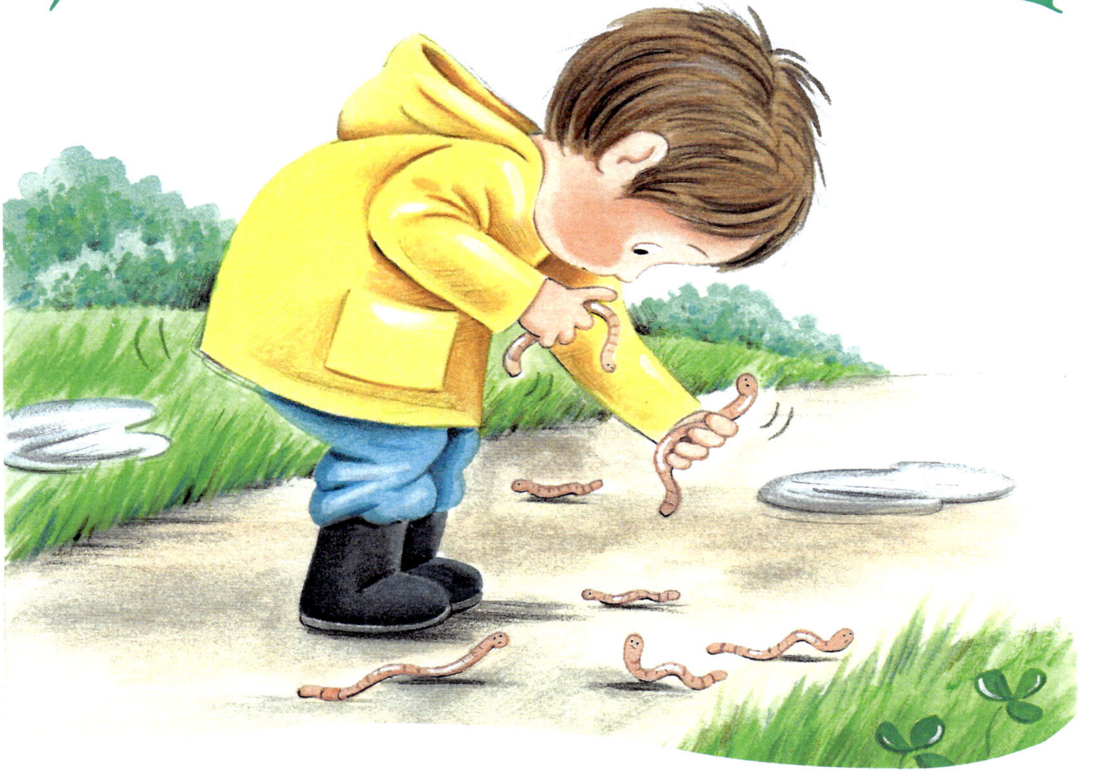

Written by TOM HEETDERKS

Illustrated by Rachel Baines

The Worm Saver

Published in the United States by Credo House Publishers
a division of Credo Communications, LLC, Grand Rapids, Michigan
credohousepublishers.com

ISBN: 978-1-62586-251-8

Illustrations by Rachel Baines
Interior design and typesetting by Sharon VanLoozenoord
Editing by Crystal Bowman

Printed in the United States of America

First edition

To my grandson, Roman.

Through pouring rain, or blazing sun,
or any kind of weather,
life is better for everyone
when we work together.

Keep saving worms!

Pitter, patter. Drip, drip, drop—
The rain poured down all day.
Dark clouds covered up the sun.
I needed boots to play.

Muddy puddles were ankle deep.
The water swirled around.
The sidewalk filled with squiggling worms
that crept up from the ground.

But while I splashed in puddles,
the clouds were swept away.
The sun shone bright in clear blue skies.
The heat was here to stay!

I looked at all the struggling worms
and wondered what to do.
I needed help to rescue them
before the day was through.

"Who can help?" I hollered out.
"Is anybody there?
We need to save these worms today!
Does anybody care?"

My neighbors were much too busy with problems of their own.

So, saving all these wiggly worms was up to me alone.

I scooped one up and placed the worm
beneath an apple tree.
But this was going to take all day
with no one helping me!

"Ruff! Ruff! Ruff!" a big old dog
barked loud as if to say,
"I cannot help you with these worms.
I've much to do today."

So, one by one I picked them up.
I hoped to save them all.
Skinny, slippery, slimy ones,
the big ones and the small.

"Meow!" A fluffy cat came by.
"Please help me, kitty cat."

She hissed at me as if to say,
"I cannot help with that!"

I held a teeny, tiny worm.
It wriggled in my hand.
"Don't worry, little worm," I said.
"You need some cooler land."

"Ribbet! Ribbet! Ribbet! Croak!"
Some frogs hopped through the grass.
"Help you pick up all these worms?
No thanks, we'll have to pass."

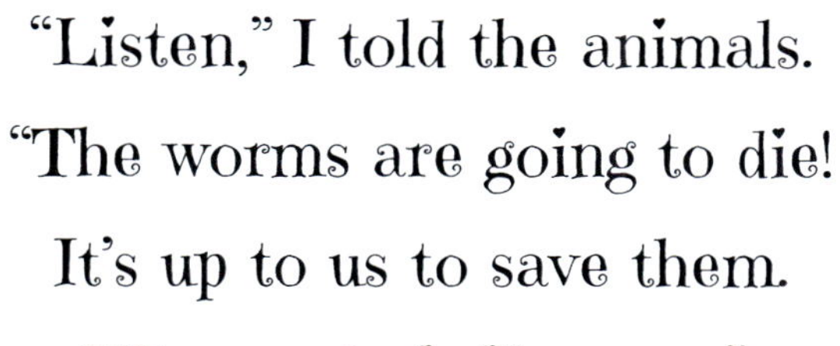

"Listen," I told the animals.
"The worms are going to die!
It's up to us to save them.
We can do it if we try."

“So why not help each little worm
and change their life today?
Just do whatever you can do
before you go away.”

The animals huddled for quite some time

and then . . .

Each one changed their mind!
They wanted to make a difference
by helping and being kind.

The dog nudged a slithering worm
as carefully as he could.
The worm rolled over once or twice
and landed where it should.

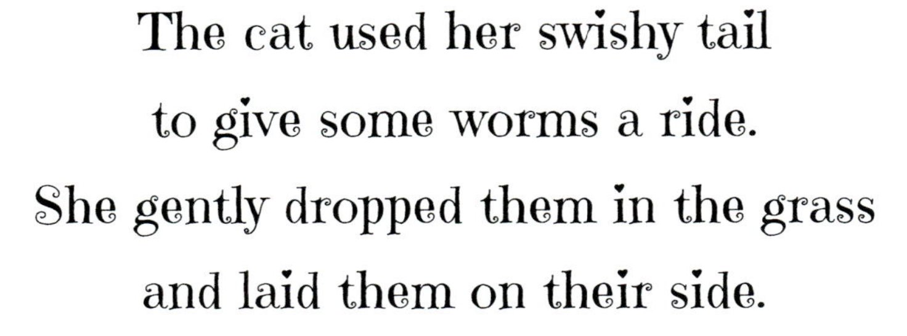

The cat used her swishy tail
to give some worms a ride.
She gently dropped them in the grass
and laid them on their side.

The frogs stuck out their sticky tongues.
They did their very best
to bring the worms into the shade
so they could stretch and rest.

“Hoorah! We did it! We saved them all!
The worms will be okay!
They’re finally back where they belong.
Oh, what a happy day!”